FRANCISCO VÁZQUEZ DE CORONADO

First European to Reach the Grand Canyon

XINA M. UHL

ROSEN
PUBLISHING®

New York

Published in 2017 by The Rosen Publishing Group, Inc.
29 East 21st Street, New York, NY 10010

First Edition

Library of Congress Cataloging-in-Publication Data

Names: Uhl, Xina M., author.
Title: Francisco Vázquez de Coronado: First European to Reach the Grand Canyon / Xina M. Uhl.
Description: First edition. | New York : Rosen Publishing, 2017 | Series:
  Spotlight on explorers and colonization | Includes bibliographical
  references and index.
Identifiers: LCCN 2016017847| ISBN 9781508172161 (library bound) | ISBN
  9781508172147 (pbk.) | ISBN 9781508172154 (6-pack)
Subjects: LCSH: Coronado, Francisco Vázquez de, 1510–1554—Juvenile
  literature. | Explorers—America—Biography—Juvenile literature. |
  Explorers—Spain—Biography—Juvenile literature. | Southwest,
  New—Discovery and exploration—Spanish—Juvenile literature. |
  America—Discovery and exploration—Spanish—Juvenile literature.
Classification: LCC E125.V3 U45 2016 | DDC 979.01092 [B] —dc23
LC record available at https://lccn.loc.gov/2016017847

Manufactured in China

CONTENTS

WAS CORONADO A SUCCESS OR FAILURE?

In 1520, a Spanish explorer sailed to Mexico. There, Hernán Cortés found the Aztecs. They had a vast, wealthy empire. When Cortés conquered it for Spain, glory and great riches were his. In 1524, a Spanish explorer came to Peru. He found the Inca Empire and conquered it. Its riches were even greater.

More wealth might yet be discovered in the New World, so Francisco Vázquez de Coronado left Spain to find it. He would make an amazing, dangerous journey. From Mexico, he went northeast all the way to Kansas. Spurred on by a myth of seven cities of gold, he traveled far

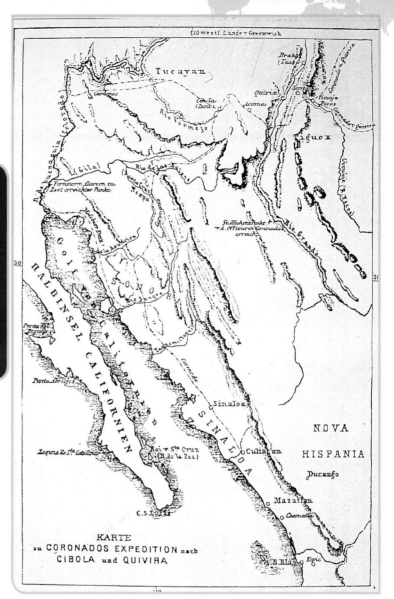

Coronado's journey northward from Mexico City is shown on this map from 1540. Today, maps of northern Mexico and the southwestern United States look much different.

to explore areas Europeans had never seen before.

He never found the gold he sought, nor did he find the precious gems. He returned to Mexico a failure. But as an explorer, he earned a place in history. You decide whether this makes him a success or failure.

AN EXPLORER IS BORN

Sometime around 1510, Francisco Vázquez de Coronado was born in Salamanca, Spain. His noble family sent him to court as a young man. There, he and Antonio de Mendoza became friends. The king favored Mendoza and made him viceroy of New Spain, an area that covered Mexico, the Caribbean islands, and most of Central America. He went to Mexico City in 1535, and twenty-five-year old Coronado joined him. While there, Coronado married the wealthy Beatriz Estrada, who brought a huge estate with her into the marriage. They went on to have five children together.

Coronado might have remained an unknown Spaniard if it weren't for his acquaintance with Antonio de Mendoza, the marquis of Mondejar, count of Tendilla, and first viceroy of New Spain.

Coronado took up the job of inspector for Mendoza. In 1537, he went to investigate a slave uprising in the mines southwest of Mexico City. The slaves were blacks and Native Americans. Coronado killed the rebellion leaders, which ended the uprising and earned him great fame as a pacifier of natives.

CORONADO'S RISE

Coronado went on to investigate other complaints for Mendoza. The viceroy was so happy with his work that the next year Mendoza appointed him the governor of New Galicia. This province lay northwest of Mexico City. It included parts of northern and western Mexico, as well as an unclear border in what is today the American Southwest. The area was remote and unexplored by the Spanish.

In that same year, 1538, Viceroy Mendoza sent a priest and a Moor out on a mission. The two, Friar Marcos de Niza and a black

slave named Estéban, traveled northwest to the town of Compostela. From there, they journeyed north for several months. Their task: find the fabled Seven Golden Cities of Cibola. Another Spanish explorer, Álvar Núñez Cabeza de Vaca, visited Mexico City. He reported that he had heard stories about huge, wealthy cities northward, which made Mendoza eager to discover if these cities really existed.

A FABULOUS TALE

Marcos de Niza returned to Mendoza alone in 1539. He reported that he and Estéban had quarreled during their travels. Estéban had traveled a few days ahead of de Niza. During that time, Native Americans had killed Estéban near the city of Hawikuh. De Niza also reported something else, too. He was certain that the Seven Golden Cities of Cibola were more than a myth, because a trusted Native American assured him they were real. Not only that, but de Niza claimed he had seen them with his own eyes in the distance. They were

The remains of Hawikuh are located 12 miles (19 kilometers) southwest of Zuni, New Mexico. At its height, the village had 125 rooms in structures that stood up to four stories tall.

large and grand with jewels, gold, and silver filling their streets.

The myth of the Seven Cities of Cibola had interested the Spanish as far back as the eighth century. Marcos de Niza's exciting report seemed to show that soon the Spanish would conquer these cities. They would have to get there first, though.

GLORY, GOD, AND GOLD

De Niza's reports delighted both Mendoza and Coronado, so they quickly decided to make a grand expedition to the north. They had three reasons for the trip. First, they wanted to conquer the area for Spain and earn glory for themselves. Second, they wanted to bring Christianity to a heathen land. Finally, they wanted to find great riches, especially gold. Such a huge journey was so expensive that Mendoza and Coronado used much of their own funds for the trip's costs. Coronado's portion came from his wife.

Mendoza appointed Coronado as the trip's leader. Because Coronado was the governor

Spanish explorers like Coronado hoped that their journey into the unknown lands of the American Southwest would bring them fame and fortune. They also wanted the natives to become Christians.

of this unexplored area, he should be the one to claim the cities and gold for Spain. Three hundred Spaniards volunteered for the quest. Eight hundred natives also joined. Many of these natives had allied with the Spanish to defeat the Aztecs in 1520. But some of them had little choice about leaving, because their Spanish overlords forced them to go.

THE JOURNEY BEGINS

Coronado traveled to the city of Compostela near Mexico's western coast. Here, the members of the expedition gathered. The group was made up of about two thousand people, which included horsemen, Native Americans, servants, and family members. A small number of women went along, too, some of whom were wives of the soldiers. The group brought herds of cattle and pigs to eat along the way. Up to a thousand extra horses came along, too. Heavy cannons were for defense.

Coronado's expedition included hundreds of people, including natives, servants, and even some wives of the soldiers. They were accompanied by supplies, equipment, weapons, and herds of livestock and horses.

In February 1540 they set off northward. Soon, they stopped at Culiacán, an outpost on the coast where Coronado separated his forces. Coronado, Marcos de Niza, and one hundred European soldiers led a few hundred Native Americans, slaves, and servants. This small group could travel quicker without the livestock. On April 22, 1540, they headed north, and from here on out the land was uninhabited. The rest of the group stayed at Culiacán to follow later.

ACROSS THE FRONTIER

The exact route Coronado followed north is not known because so little evidence of it has been left behind for scholars to study. Still, we do know some facts. After around a month, they crossed the Gila River, which is located in modern western New Mexico. They continued across the Colorado River plateau. They named areas they came across, often using names from native words for places. They passed pine forests and mountains.

Some of Coronado's party rode horseback while others walked. Father de Niza had claimed that the way was easy, but

The Gila River flows southwest across present-day Arizona into New Mexico. During the months Coronado would have crossed it the weather would have been quite hot.

most lacked de Niza's experience walking long distances. Four months later, on July 7, 1540, they came upon the first city of Cibola. They expected to find the famed city of gold and gems. Instead, they found a small crowded village called Hawikuh, made of adobe. The Zuni Pueblo natives did not wear rich clothing. In fact, riches were nowhere to be found.

THE FIRST BATTLE

The sight of Hawikuh did more than disappoint Coronado's men, it angered them. Had de Niza lied to them about the golden cities? It seemed so.

For the Zuni people, it was the time of summer ceremonies. They had gathered there from seven villages. Smoke rose from their fires. They held weapons and blew horns. Coronado sent a small party of men forward. By Spanish law, they had to read a statement to them called the Requerimiento, which informed them that they were under Spanish rule. They must now accept that and become Christians.

The Zuni people were participating in a summer solstice ritual like the one shown here when Coronado arrived.

If they did not, they would be killed or become slaves.

When the natives shot arrows at Coronado and his men, a battle began. A huge stone hit Coronado and wounded him. The Spanish had better weapons, and their horseback riders also gave them an advantage. Soon, they entered the pueblo. The Zuni fled.

THE REAL CIBOLA

Inside the pueblo, the Spaniards found food. This was a welcome find, because their supplies had dwindled during their trip, leaving them hungry. When they searched the homes and buildings, however, rather than gold they found blankets and turquoise.

Coronado claimed that he ordered the Zuni to be treated well. The women, children, and elderly had fled Hawikuh before the battle, and Coronado asked the Zuni leaders to bring their people back. Although he promised special protection for women and children, they remained hidden. After some discussion, the Spanish traded a

Native American buildings, like the Zuni pueblo shown here, were constructed out of materials from the surrounding land. Mud, clay, and straw were formed into bricks that were dried in the sun.

few goods with the Zuni for blankets, bows and arrows, and turquoise.

What about Marcos de Niza's tales of gold and silver? They were all lies. Coronado sent a report back to Mendoza. About de Niza he wrote, "I can assure you ... he has not told a single truth in what he said." De Niza returned to Mexico in disgrace. His untruths gave him a nickname: the "liar friar."

TRAVELING ON

Coronado had his men search the seven towns around Hawikuh, which he renamed Granada. None of them contained the kind of riches he desired. Unwilling to give up yet, the determined explorer sent out a party of men to investigate tales of red mountains split by a great river. This group became the first white men to see Arizona's Grand Canyon.

Meanwhile, Coronado and the main army traveled east. He sent out another party, this one under Hernando de Alvarado, which traveled for eighty days. They passed a large pueblo village named Ácoma, but they

Ácoma Pueblo is built atop a bluff, or mesa, that is more than 300 feet (91 meters) tall. "Mesa" means "table" in Spanish. The Spanish thought such hills resembled tabletops.

continued onward as far as the Pecos River in Texas. Along the way they gathered a herd of buffalo. A Pawnee native captive called the Turk herded the buffalo and also told them stories of a place further east called Quivira. There they would find gold, silver, and fine fabrics, he said.

THE TIGEUX WAR

In the meantime, Coronado's main army stopped for the winter of 1540. This was in the Rio Grande valley at a place called Tigeux. Today it is near Santa Fe, New Mexico. Tigeux had between twelve and twenty pueblos. More people lived there than in Granada. The climate was mild and food was plentiful.

At first, the Spanish and the Native Americans at Tigeux were friendly. That quickly changed as Spanish demands for food, clothing, and housing angered the natives. The natives then attacked the Spanish horses, killing about sixty, and warfare broke out. The Spanish won easily,

This kiva is built at the Tigeux Pueblo in New Mexico. A kiva is a round room that is used for ceremonies. A hole in the roof serves as a doorway.

and they pledged peace. Coronado wanted to keep the natives from defying the Spanish, however, so he burned several hundred natives at the stake.

The winter was long and hard for the Spanish, who were hungry and cold. Although they tried to trade for food, the Native Americans refused. They no longer trusted the Spanish.

FABLED QUIVIRA

In the spring of 1541, Coronado left to search for Quivira, taking with him the Turk as his guide as well as thirty men. They headed east through the Texas Panhandle. The area they entered is now known as the Great Plains. Mile after mile they saw nothing but flat plains without trees, hills, or roads. Men who went out to hunt often got lost trying to find their way back. One man and two horses never did return.

The great herds of bison thundering across the land provided the Spanish with all the food they needed. Wolf packs followed the bison, as did the Native

Coronado's men often wore heavy plate armor on their chests and arms and as helmets. They carried lances, crossbows, and swords.

Americans. The natives they met were mostly Apaches. The Apaches had never seen horses before, but in later years, Native Americans would become skilled horsemen.

Coronado and his men continued on, first turning north through Oklahoma and then advancing into central Kansas. At last they came to Quivira, near present-day Salina.

THE END OF THE LINE

In June 1541, Coronado and his men arrived in Quivira. Here they expected to find gold and silver. They had come so far, surely they would find what they sought at last.

Quivira contained only natives' teepees. The Plains Indians who lived in them hunted buffalo. They also planted cornfields. Quivira's role in trade made it important for Native Americans, but without riches and treasures, the Europeans found only disappointment there.

Finally, the Turk admitted that he had lied to the explorer. He said his masters had told him to lead the Spanish away. He was to

The Turk served as a guide for the Spanish as they traveled through the barren Great Plains in search of Quivira.

lead them to barren areas without water and food. Then he should leave them there to die. Coronado had the Turk killed for his lies. Some Native Americans today consider the Turk a hero. They believe that he led the Spanish astray to save his people from the harm the Spanish might cause.

BACK TO THE RIO GRANDE

At last, Coronado gave up his plan to head farther north. He stayed in Quivira for twenty-five days, then in late August 1541 he left. Most of his men went with him. Only a priest and a few others stayed behind. As soon as Coronado's army left, the natives killed the priest. A European named Campo survived and made his way back to Mexico by himself.

Coronado guided his army back to Tigeux. They moved quickly. On October 2, 1541, they arrived back in the Rio Grande pueblos. The army stayed through that winter. The Native Americans were still unfriendly, and in the Spanish camp the men

Coronado passed through south central Kansas on the search for Quivira. Today the region includes the Quivira National Wildlife Refuge, where salt marshes provide cover for migratory birds.

quarreled with each other. Regular soldiers resented the officers, who ate better food and took the best clothing for themselves. The men spent the winter hungry and wearing clothing that was in tatters. They had been traveling in the same clothes for two years.

WHAT NEXT?

Coronado heard more rumors about large towns further east. He wanted to return to Quivira in the spring of 1542. Then they could learn more about these villages. Bad news came from New Spain, though. A large native revolt known as the Mixtón War was going on in New Galicia. The Spanish won it in 1542. Between this war and the hostility of the natives in Tigeux, Coronado thought twice about this plan.

Then Coronado fell off his horse and seriously injured his head. For a while no one thought he would survive. He did recover in time, though.

Coronado did not want to admit that his journey had been a failure. He had not found

Coronado wanted to travel on after the failure at Quivira, but problems back in New Spain kept him from doing so.

any gold, so the money he and Mendoza had used to fund the expedition would not be recovered. Still, he missed his family, and he missed Mexico City. He decided to give up and return home.

HEADING HOME

In April 1542 Coronado and his army left Tigeux and headed south toward Mexico. Many hardships dogged them. Summer heat and illness made them miserable. Native attacks put them in danger. The soldiers resisted following orders, quarrels broke out, and some men deserted the army.

Scholars do not know the exact route Coronado took home. Their route probably passed Dodge City, Kansas. Heading south, they went through the panhandles of Oklahoma and Texas. Other cities they may have passed through include Amarillo,

Vast herds of bison roamed the Great Plains before the coming of the Spanish. Native Americans were able to hunt them more efficiently after obtaining horses from the Spanish.

Texas; Albuquerque, New Mexico; and Sierra Vista, Arizona.

Coronado's force split up once they entered New Galicia. When he arrived in Mexico City he had just one hundred soldiers. Others followed later, though. Many of them did not return at all. They settled near Mexican cities like Compostela. The shame of returning to Mexico City as failures was too much for them.

From start to finish, Coronado's journey was more than 4,000 miles (6,437 kilometers).

BACK IN MEXICO

Coronado and his men returned to Mexico in defeat. Viceroy Mendoza had been the biggest investor in the expedition. Now he had nothing to show for his money. Coronado tried to resign as governor of New Galicia in 1543, but in 1544 Mendoza appointed him as governor again. He and his officers soon found themselves in court. They had to explain the failure of their journey. Coronado also had to account for the Native Americans he had killed. He was found not guilty on most charges.

His troubles were not over, though. He lost his position as governor after

On the trip back to Mexico the explorers not only had to deal with miserably hot weather, but also the knowledge that they were returning home without the riches they had sought.

accusations of misconduct. Next he returned to Mexico City where he became a member of the city council. His legal battles went on. One involved his *encomienda*. This grant allowed him to require the natives on his estate to be enslaved. It also required him to teach them to become Christians.

AN UNTIMELY END

The lawsuit over Coronado's encomienda was still pending in 1554. On September 22, ten years after his epic journey, he died suddenly at the age of forty-three. The cause of death was an illness that other city council members also suffered from. He was buried in Mexico City at the Santo Domingo Church. His wife Beatriz never remarried, but instead she devoted herself to pious work in the church.

Coronado failed to find empires of gold and gems, but of course they did not exist. Thanks to his expedition, the Spanish learned about the foreign land

Francisco Vásquez de Coronado died young and without finding the glory he had hoped for, but the memory of his epic journey has lingered on.

beyond New Spain. It paved the way for later explorers to return and establish European settlements. This Hispanic culture remains in the Southwest today.

THE NATIVE VIEW

Francisco Vázquez de Coronado was just one of many Spanish explorers who made their way across North America and significantly changed the lives of the Native Americans. Their Christian religion affected native beliefs, for example. The introduction of horses changed how they hunted and made war. But their exposure also meant terrible losses for the natives. More than 50 percent of Native Americans died from disease carried by the Europeans. They also lost their land bit by bit, and today, selected tribes live on scattered reservations. Over time, their whole way of life came to an end.

Spaniards like Coronado were the first to bring change to the Native American tribes who dwelled in North America, but they would not be the last.

Three centuries after Coronado's journey home, the Santa Fe Trail may have followed his route. In recognition of his long journey, Coronado's name has been given to many places, schools, and parks across North America. His quest did not bring the results he hoped for, but today's world would have been far different without his efforts.

GLOSSARY

adobe A clay made of earth dried by the sun.

barren Poor soil that grows few plants.

bison A large mammal with a shaggy coat, huge head, short curving horns, and a hump on its back. They are sometimes called buffalo.

deserted To have left a place, position, or individual.

dogged To pursue an ideal or person stubbornly.

dwindled To have become less than it once was.

estate A large home on a big piece of land, often in the countryside.

heathen Someone who does not belong to a popular religion, such as Christianity.

livestock Farm animals that are used or sold.

Moor A person from North Africa who usually followed the religion of Islam.

New World Referring to the area of North and South America, especially by early European explorers.

pacifier Something that keeps people calm.

pending Something that is not yet accomplished.

pious Extremely religious.

plateau A large, flat area of high elevation.

pledged To have promised to do something.

pueblo A Native American village with adobe homes joined together, which can be several stories tall.

reservations Areas of land set aside for certain Native American tribes to live on.

sought Having gone in search of something.

Autry Museum of the American West
4700 Western Heritage Way
Los Angeles, CA 90027-1462
(323) 667-2000
Website: http://theautry.org
The art, history, and cultures of the American West
 are featured at the Autry Museum. The highlights
 of changing museum exhibitions can be accessed
 through this site, as well as online research tools.

Buffalo Bill Center of the West
720 Sheridan Avenue
Cody, WY 82414
(307) 587-4771
Website: https://centerofthewest.org
The Buffalo Bill Center of the West is affiliated with
 the Smithsonian Institute. Its website includes
 interactive online media such as blog posts,
 videos, and photographs. Also featured are
 interesting essays on well-known Western figures,
 both early in the country's history and later.

The Library of Congress
101 Independence Ave SE
Washington, DC 20540
(202) 707-5000
Website: http://www.loc.gov

The American history section of this site contains
an extensive catalog on "the Americas to 1620."
Multiple collections reveal American history in art,
documents, and artifacts.

National Humanities Center
7 T. W. Alexander Drive
PO Box 12256
Research Triangle Park, NC 27709
(919) 549-0661
Website: http://americainclass.org/primary-sources
This site collects a number of important primary sources
from different time periods in American history. Under
the exploration tab of "American beginnings: the
European presence in North America: 1492–1690"
you will find a number of documents, reading guides,
and helpful questions. Each entry is designed to
make this time in history come alive through the eyes
of the people who lived it.

Websites

Because of the changing nature of internet links, Rosen
Publishing has developed an online list of websites
related to the subject of this book. This site is updated
regularly. Please use this link to access the list:

http://www.rosenlinks.com/SEC/coro

Aronson, Marc. *The World Made New: Why the Age of Exploration Happened and How It Changed the World.* New York, NY: National Geographic Children's Books, 2007.

Burgan, Michael. *New World Explorers: The Story of North American's First Explorers.* North Mankato, MN: Capstone Press, 2016.

Cunningham, Kevin. *The Pueblo.* New York, NY: Scholastic, 2011.

Matthews, Rupert. *Conquistadors.* New York, NY: Gareth Stevens Publishing, 2015.

Patent, Dorothy Hinshaw. *The Horse and the Plains Indians: A Powerful Partnership.* New York, NY: Clarion Books, 2012

Perritano, John. *Spanish Missions.* New York, NY: Children's Press, 2010.

Petrie, Kristin. *Francisco Vásquez De Coronado.* Bel Air, CA: Checkerboard Library, 2004.

Pletcher, Kenneth. *The Age of Exploration.* New York, NY: Britannica Educational Publishing, 2014.

Roberts, Steven. *Francisco Vásquez De Coronado.* New York, NY: PowerKids Press, 2013.

Santella, Andrew. *Plains Indians.* Portsmouth, NH: Heinemann, 2011.

BIBLIOGRAPHY

"Coronado's Exploration Into the Southwest: Cast of Characters." Planetary Science Institute, 2016 (https//www.psi.edu/about/staff/hartmann /coronado/castofcharacters.html).

"Coronado's Seven Cities Continued." United States National Park Service. Retrieved April 9, 2016 (https://www.nps.gov/coro/learn/historyculture /coronados-seven-cities-continued.htm).

Donoghue, David. "Coronado Expedition." *The Handbook of Texas* online. Texas State Historical Association, June 12, 2010 (https://tshaonline.org /handbook/online/articles/upcpt).

Flint, Richard, and Shirley Cushing Flint. "People." New Mexico Office of the State Historian. Retrieved April 7, 2016 (http://newmexicohistory .org/people/francisco-vazquez-de-coronado).

"Francisco Vázquez De Coronado." PBS: New Perspectives on the West, 2001 (https://www.pbs .org/weta/thewest/people/a_c/coronado.htm).

"How the European Conquest Affected Native Americans." Phys.org, January 24, 2012 (http:// phys.org/news/2012-01-european-conquest -affected-native-americans.html).

Lewis, Tom, and Sara Jean Richter. "Coronado Expedition." *Encyclopedia of Oklahoma History and Culture* online, 2009 (http://www.okhistory.org /publications/enc/entry.php?entry=CO062).

INDEX

About the Author

Xina M. Uhl discovered her love of history while still in grade school. She went on to obtain a master of arts in history from California State University, Northridge, with a focus on the Ancient Mediterranean. After teaching college-level American history, she moved into educational writing. She has authored books, textbooks, teacher's guides, lessons, and assessment questions in the field of history. She makes her home in sunny Southern California, where she spends far too much time reading. When she is not writing she enjoys travel, photography, and hiking with her dogs. Her blog features her travel adventures and latest fiction projects.

Photo Credits